# SUSTAINABLE
# HOMES

## by Ewan McLeish

**Smart Apple Media**

HERR MEMORIAL LIBRARY

First published in 2006 by Evans Brothers Limited
2A Portman Mansions, Chiltern Street, London W1U 6NR

Produced for Evans Brothers Limited by White-Thomson Publishing Ltd.
210 High Street, Lewes, East Sussex BN7 2NH

This edition published under license from Evans Brothers Limited. All rights reserved.
Copyright © 2006 White-Thomas Publishing Ltd.

Editorial: Catherine Clarke; Design: Tinstar Design Ltd.; Consultant: Greta Jensen;
WWF Reviewers: Patricia Kendell and Cherry Duggan; Picture Research: Amy Sparks

Acknowledgements
Alamy **pp. 7**, **15**, **37**, **44**; Biolet Composting Toilets **p. 27**; Corbis **pp. 6** (Les Stone), **14** (The Cover Story), **18** (Richard Hamilton Smith), **20** (Lester Lefkowitz), **23** (Reuters), **26** (Ecoscene), **29** (ChromoSohm Inc.), **30** (Roger Ressmeyer), **35** (Gary Braasch), **39** (Craig Lovell), **38** (Edifice), **41** (Robert Llewellyn), **42** (Christine Muschi), **45** (Joseph Sohm/ChromoSohm Inc.); Ecoscene **pp. 4** (Bruce Harber), **5** (Martin Jones), **13** (Barry Hughes), **16** (Tony Page), **25** (Stephen Coyne), **28** (John Wilkinson), **40** (Paul Thompson), **43** (Tony Page); Photolibrary **pp. 9** (OSF), **10** (Workbook Inc.), **11** (Robin Smith), **22** (Phototake Inc.), **31** (Index Stock Imagery), **32** (BSIP), **33** (OSF), **34** (Clive Nichols), **36** (OSF); Practical Action ITDG **pp. 12** (Zul), **19** (Jean Long); Topfoto **pp. 8** (The Image Works), **17** (Keystone); Waste Watch/Recycle Now **p. 24**.

Cover image courtesy of Bruce Harber/Ecoscene.

World Wildlife Fund-UK Registered Charity No. 1081247. A company limited by guarantee number 4016725.
Panda symbol © 1986 WWF. ® WWF Registered trademark.

Published in the United States by Smart Apple Media
2140 Howard Drive West, North Mankato, Minnesota 56003

U.S. publication copyright © 2007 Smart Apple Media
International copyright reserved in all countries. No part of this book may be reproduced in any form without written permission from the publisher.
Printed in China

Library of Congress Cataloging-in-Publishing Data

McLeish, Ewan, 1950-
Sustainable homes / by Ewan McLeish.
p. cm. — (Sustainable futures)
Includes index.
ISBN-13: 978-1-58340-982-4
1. Ecological houses—Juvenile literature. 2. Housing—Environmental aspects—Juvenile literature.
3. Dwellings—Energy conservation—Juvenile literature. 4. Urban ecology—Juvenile literature.
5. Environmental management—Juvenile literature. I. Title II. Series.

HD7287.M422 2006
690'.8047—dc22          2005057612

9 8 7 6 5 4 3 2 1

# Contents

# No place like home?

We all need shelter of some kind. Shelter protects us from the elements, keeps us warm (or cool), and gives us a feeling of security. But most of us need more than that. We don't just want to feel safe or warm, we want to belong and feel like part of a community. We want somewhere we can call home.

## The impact of homes

Our homes affect us, but they also affect our surroundings, or environment, both directly and indirectly. How they look and how and where they are built all have an impact on our surroundings. But they have a much wider impact, too. At home, we consume huge quantities of resources such as energy and water. These are the things we use as part of our everyday lives. Obtaining and using these resources can be highly damaging to the environment. Nearly a third of the total energy used in most European countries goes into homes. In the United States, the figure is about 20 percent. In many developing countries, the proportion is far higher, although they use much less energy overall. This is because they depend more on agriculture than industry. In India, for example, 91 percent of all energy used in the country goes into homes. As these developing countries become more industrialized, however, this is likely to change.

This dome eco-house has been built using recycled or natural materials, such as wood, that have come from a sustainable source. Energy is supplied by solar panels and a wind turbine. The dome shape reduces heat loss and the use of building materials by 30 percent.

Our daily activities are also responsible for producing large amounts of waste. Some of it takes years, even centuries, to break down. Some of these wastes are toxic, particularly when burned. Others can be harmful for different reasons. Many of the chemicals we use in the home are toxic and may have long-term damaging effects, both for people and the environment.

## A sustainable home?

We all want to feel comfortable and secure in our homes. But that doesn't have to create a massive impact on the environment. We can make our homes great places to live without "costing Earth." Perhaps more importantly, doing this may mean that our children, and their children, can do the same. This is what is meant by sustainable living.

This house in Kathmandu Valley is built of natural local materials, including the thatched roof made from straw.

## Different lives—different sustainable homes

David lives on a housing estate in the United Kingdom (UK). From the outside, the houses look normal, but when you look closer, you can see that parts of the roof are covered with dark panels. These are solar heaters that use the energy of the sun to heat water. Inside, you become aware of a slight hum. This is a low-speed fan, drawing in air through the roof, improving ventilation and reducing moisture. As you look around, you notice that the light bulbs look strange. The more you look, the more you can see that this is not an ordinary house at all. It is a sustainable home.

Kerry's house doesn't look normal, even from the outside. It juts out, like a huge, steel-clad wedge from granite boulders, overlooking a bay in Nova Scotia. At the center of the living space is a sky-lit courtyard that helps control conditions within the house, creating its own microclimate. Windows on the east side of the house are larger than on the west and allow in more light and less heat in the summer. Much of the structure is made from local materials, and the design matches the rugged landscape into which it is built. It is also a sustainable home.

Vaneeta's home is near Durban in Kwa-Zulu Natal Province, South Africa. Hers is one of more than 6,000 homes built by the residents themselves under a national government project. Mud bricks conserve heat at night and keep rooms cool during the day. The project also uses natural features, making use of local plants and the natural slopes and drainage to filter water. Vaneeta lives in a sustainable home, too.

# Sustainable development

Living sustainably means providing for our needs without damaging the environment or the ability of others to meet their own needs, both now and in the future. Applying this to all aspects of how we live, including our homes, is known as sustainable development.

## Quality of life

The idea of sustainable development goes much farther than using resources wisely or protecting our surroundings. It is about the way we live, which is sometimes called "quality of life," too. There is a close link between the quality of people's homes and their quality of life. For example, poor-quality or inadequate housing is often linked to a lack of resources or facilities in the area. This may in turn be linked to poverty, unemployment, and even poor health. Sustainable housing can reverse this process by linking good-quality housing to work and training opportunities and good local services (such as stores, schools, and transportation). The homes themselves, in the way they are built and operate, can help create healthy living conditions. In this way, people's health and well-being are linked to the health and well-being of the environment.

A poor Haitian couple stands with their child in the doorway of a rundown shack that is their home. Poor-quality homes like this contribute to other problems, such as poor health.

There are several programs around the world involved with building eco-homes. These volunteers in Wales are building a straw bale house using natural materials as part of a project set up by the Center for Alternative Technology.

## Eco-homes

"EcoHomes" is an example of a project that gives some idea of what is involved in sustainable homes. This UK program rates homes on their sustainability. It balances environmental issues, such as resource use and impact on wildlife, against the need for affordable, high-quality, safe, and healthy homes. Homes are judged on:

- energy
- public transportation links
- pollution
- use of materials
- water use
- land use
- ecology
- the health and well-being of the inhabitants.

Each of these areas has a score attached to it. The scores combine to form a rating, and the goal is to achieve a "good" or "better" rating for all new and refurbished homes from 2005 onward.

## Case Study: Tlholego eco-village

The Tlholego eco-village is situated on half a square mile (1.5 sq km) in the northwest province of South Africa. It was established in 1991 in order to provide a rural "living and learning center" involving poor workers and unemployed city-dwellers. Homes are owner-built using low-cost methods and building materials, such as ferro-cement, that do little damage to the environment. Ferro-cement is strong but lightweight and uses smaller amounts of cement than normal concrete. This avoids the poor quality and environmental problems of normal, low-cost housing. Tlholego also trains people in the design and setup of sustainable village communities, including a farm school for 250 students from the surrounding community. In 2000, the village was chosen by the National Department of Housing as a "model representing South Africa's solutions toward sustainable development."

## Different places, different homes

Different environments require different measures to achieve sustainability. For example, in much of northern Europe and North America, the need to keep homes warm during a large part of the year means that energy-saving measures are of major importance. In warmer climates, keeping cool is usually of more importance.

## Fitting in

Sustainable homes should also make use of local building materials and fit in with the local landscape. The location of a sustainable home will determine the choice of materials used, such as timber, stone, or earth, according to what is available locally.

## Homegrown

In Mali, Guinea, many of the houses have thatched roofs that match the slope of the landscape. The eastern side of these houses is constructed of woven bamboo. The remaining walls are built of stabilized rammed (compressed) earth, rather than "fired" bricks. Brick kilns, needed to harden normal bricks, are banned in Mali because they burn wood, which leads to deforestation. Making rammed earth bricks, using a hand-operated press, is an ancient skill in Guinea. Now the technology has been adapted by stabilizing the soil with small amounts of cement to make the bricks stronger. Roof tiles are made in the same way, but fiber from locally grown plants, rather than cement, is used to stabilize the tiles.

Bricks made of mud or earth that is rammed together, or compressed, and dried in the sun are a more sustainable option than fired bricks from a kiln.

Part of a rain forest cleared for farming in Madagascar. Poor people often have no choice but to damage their environment to obtain the resources they need or to make a living.

## Rich and poor

In the developing world, such as parts of Africa and Asia, people often have no choice but to live unsustainably. They may be forced to damage their environment—by clearing forests, for example—in order to survive. Much of the deforestation in these areas, however, is caused by developers clearing land to grow crops or graze cattle. In the developed countries of Europe and North America, most people live unsustainably in a different way, by consuming too many resources and creating pollution. The idea of sustainable homes will therefore have different meanings in these different situations.

There are also differences between rural and urban communities. In developing countries, many people move from rural areas into cities to look for work. This often puts enormous pressure on urban resources such as energy and clean water. Developing more sustainable ways of rural living can encourage people to stay in rural areas and slow the movement into cities. This may be through developing better agricultural methods or using natural forest products, such as fruits, nuts, natural cosmetics, and medicines, as a source of income. Where the technology, such as

Internet access, is available, small businesses or service industries can also do well. By relieving the pressure on urban resources and making rural living more sustainable, both areas become more environmentally friendly.

In developed and some developing countries, more people live in towns and cities, and those who don't often commute to urban areas to work. This could change. As more people in rural areas begin to use their homes as workplaces, via computers with Internet access, or set up their own local businesses, the pressure on city environments is reduced. This may result in less reliance on cars and other services, reducing the impact on resources such as fuel.

## Footprints on Earth

We live in a world in which enormous inequalities and differences exist. Even with these inequalities, we are still using far more resources than Earth can sustain. No matter where we live, sustainable homes should be about reducing our own impact, or footprint, on Earth, while allowing others a fairer share.

# The energy-saving home

We need energy to live and work. Only when energy is converted from one form to another—for example, from the chemical energy in oil to the heat energy in a boiler—can work take place. When an energy conversion takes place, some energy is always wasted. This is important in understanding ideas about the energy-saving home.

We live in an energy-hungry world that relies heavily on fossil fuels (coal, oil, and gas). We may have another 30 years of oil left in the ground and 50 years of gas if we go on using them at the present rate. Coal will last a lot longer, but its use is more damaging to the environment. We know that burning any fossil fuel produces waste gases that are harmful to the environment. The most significant of these is carbon dioxide, which is a greenhouse gas. Greenhouse gases cause warming of Earth's atmosphere by absorbing energy that radiates from Earth's surface. Although this is a natural process, increases in carbon dioxide levels in the last 100 years have produced an additional warming effect. Many people believe that this is now affecting our global climate, causing sea levels to rise.

## The energy trap

There is another problem, too. Many people simply cannot afford or obtain the fuel they need to keep warm or cook their food. Even in the richer parts of the world, people can become ill or die of cold (or dampness) due to lack of heating. In poorer regions, people may be forced to clear forests and woodlands in search of firewood to cook with. Alternatively, they may have to burn animal dung, which means wasting a valuable fertilizer. All these people are trapped in what is called "energy poverty."

An adult and child carry firewood home in Guatemala, Central America. As forests are cleared, people must travel farther to find fuel. This means that less time is available for work or for children to go to school.

## Finding the right fuel for the job

In the developed world, most household energy is used to heat water or the home itself (space heating), often by electricity. Electricity is an expensive and wasteful way of heating air or water because there are already large energy losses during its generation in power stations. Heating directly by oil is better because there are fewer energy conversions. Gas heating, using what are known as condensing boilers, is more energy efficient still (and less polluting), as long as gas is available.

### Combined heat and power

Combined heat and power (CHP), also known as cogeneration, is an efficient technology in which the heat produced during the generation of electricity is recovered and used for industrial purposes, public buildings, recreation complexes, and community heating. CHP can achieve a 35 percent reduction in energy use compared with power stations and heat-only boilers. Micro-CHP involves a small generator, about the size of a normal boiler, which provides heat and power to a single home or small residential block.

A dragline used to obtain coal from a surface mine in Australia. Many countries rely heavily on coal to meet their energy needs. Coal produces more polluting gases than either oil or natural gas, although all of these fossil fuels produce carbon dioxide when they burn.

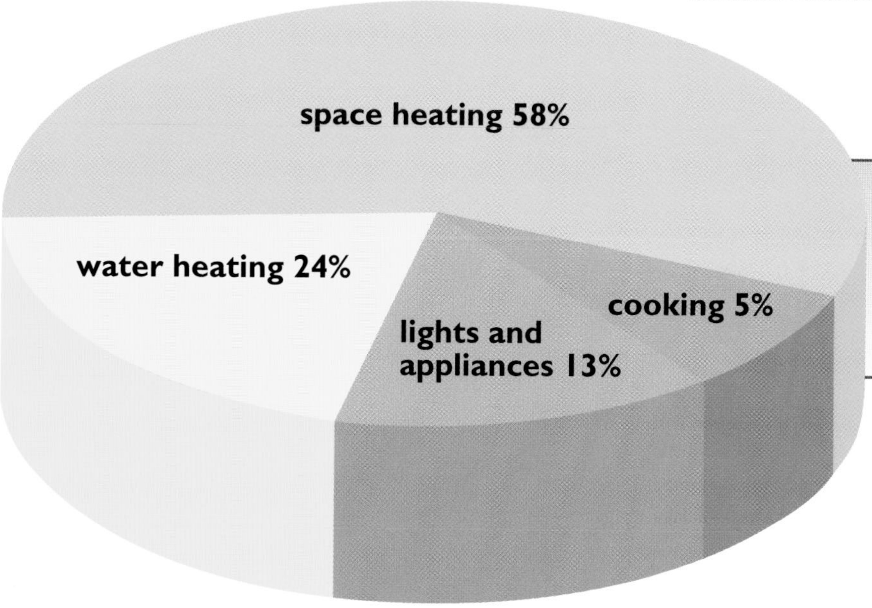

- space heating 58%
- water heating 24%
- lights and appliances 13%
- cooking 5%

This pie chart shows a breakdown of energy use in a typical home in northwest Europe. In many poorer, developing countries, most domestic energy is used for cooking.

Source: Renewable Energy: Power for a Sustainable Future, OUP 2004.

## Biomass fuels

An important source of energy, particularly in developing countries, is biomass. Biomass fuels are solid, liquid, or gas fuels produced from animal or plant material such as agricultural waste or dung. Solid biomass fuels, such as straw and wood, may be burned to generate electricity or to provide heating directly, often as part of a local CHP project. Unlike fossil fuels, biomass fuels can be described as "carbon neutral." This means that the carbon dioxide produced when the fuel burns is balanced by the carbon dioxide that was absorbed by the plant material when it was growing. In theory, therefore, it does not contribute to global warming, as there is no overall addition to carbon dioxide levels. This is only true, of course, if the fuel is replaced at the same rate as it is used up. In the case of wood, this often does not happen because trees are not always replanted. In fact, the widespread use of firewood in many regions of the world, particularly Africa and Asia, is a major cause of deforestation, as trees are cut down for heating and cooking purposes.

Most biomass fuels can also be described as renewable because there is a continuous supply of the raw materials needed to make the fuel. Again, however, this only applies to wood if new trees are planted to replace those used.

## Biogas

Gas biomass fuels, or biogas, are produced by fermenting specially grown crops (such as sugarcane or maize) or animal, human, or plant waste. In poor or isolated communities, small biogas fermenters use straw and other waste material to produce a continuous supply of gas fuel. In India, there are more than three million small biogas units, but they are unsuitable for urban environments for reasons of space and safety. Larger, community biogas plants can be more efficient, but it is sometimes difficult to balance ownership of the materials used (such as animal dung) and the amount of biogas made available to each member of the community.

This biogas fermenter in Bandarawella, Sri Lanka, has been supplying most of the energy needs of this family's home since 2000. Biogas production involves chaneling cow manure to a closed storage tank, where it breaks down and releases methane. The gas is then piped into the home to use as fuel.

Solar water heaters provide energy to this lodge in Kenya. This reduces the dependence on nonrenewable energy sources such as oil or local fuels such as wood. Technology such as this can be used to provide energy for homes, making them more sustainable.

Biogas is an enormously important energy source in the search for more sustainable homes. Its use in poorer regions such as Africa and India can reduce dependence on wood, which in turn decreases pressure on forests. Similarly, it can reduce the need for fossil fuels. In addition, the remaining slurry inside the fermenters forms a valuable fertilizer for crops.

## Doing it the renewable way

There are many other sources of renewable energy, most notably the sun and wind. Solar water heaters, usually mounted on roofs, use the sun's rays to heat water that is circulating in copper pipes on black, insulated plates.

Solar heaters work in both direct sunlight and overcast conditions and can provide 50 to 70 percent of a typical European household's hot water. In Kenya, there are about one and a half million square feet (140,000 sq m) of solar heating panels, mainly used for domestic water heating. It is estimated that with better support for solar energy, almost four and a half million square feet (400,000 sq km) of solar panels could be installed. This would reduce Kenya's annual oil imports by four percent, with a savings of around $30 million.

## Electricity from the sun

Sunlight can generate electricity directly or charge batteries using photovoltaic (PV) cells. A typical household PV array can generate around one and a half kilowatts. In a developed country, that's about a third of an average family's electricity demand. In poorer countries, such as India, photovoltaic cells are widely used to power lanterns, street lighting, and market stalls, and for pumping water for drinking and irrigation. Because they are portable, they have even been used to provide power for lanterns in a Tibetan nomad's tent!

## Case Study: Solar energy in the Auroville township

The Auroville township in India uses a variety of solar technologies to heat both water and food. Small solar ovens heat food using sunlight reflected from an angled mirror. Their use reduces reliance on bottled gas, which is expensive and contributes to global warming. Larger designs are more efficient, however.

In Auroville, a 50-foot-diameter (15 m) curved dish, built of thousands of mirrors, concentrates enough of the sun's energy to heat water to cook 2,000 meals a day!

Buildings also make use of what is known as passive solar design. Natural lighting, good ventilation, shading of walls, and good insulation of roofs create cool "comfort zones" within buildings during the heat of the day.

This giant solar dish provides power for the Auroville township by harnessing the sun's energy.

Domestic wind turbines supply electricity to this Danish community. Wind power is a renewable, nonpolluting energy source, although noise and so-called visual pollution can be a disadvantage.

## Passive solar design

Trapping the sun's energy does not necessarily require special equipment. Passive solar design involves the careful planning of buildings so that they make maximum use of the sun's energy. This can be achieved by building "solar stores." These are spaces within the building, with glass exteriors, that work in a similar way to greenhouses. Installing the largest windows in the best-lit (south-facing in the northern hemisphere and north-facing in the southern hemisphere) walls has a similar effect.

In addition, houses can be built of materials, such as concrete, stone, and earth, with high "thermal mass." This means that they heat up slowly during the day but retain the heat and allow it to escape slowly back into the house at night. In the eco-village of Tlholego, in rural South Africa, this type of passive solar technology saves residents up to 50 or 60 percent in energy costs.

## Wind power

Although large, commercial wind turbines are used throughout the world to generate electricity, smaller, community-based turbines are also an important source of locally generated energy. This is especially true in poor or isolated communities. Like solar energy, wind-generated power does not produce greenhouse gases. Small wind turbines also avoid some of the disadvantages, such as noise, land use, and "visual pollution," of the larger turbines used in wind farms. Small turbines are, however, less efficient. In Denmark, 38 percent of wind turbines are owned and operated by local communities. In India, simple wind turbines raise water from tube wells. These are wells that are drilled to reach water deep underground. Pumps are therefore needed to raise the water to the surface. Wind turbines are as effective as diesel-powered pumps but do less damage to the environment and do not rely on a supply of oil.

## Moving air

Good ventilation helps control temperatures by regulating the flow of air and reducing drafts. This, in turn, reduces the amount of energy needed for heating or air-conditioning. It also cuts down dampness due to condensation caused by moist, warm air meeting colder air. In positive pressure ventilation, a slow-speed fan in the ceiling draws in air from outside through the roof. This pushes out moisture-laden air and replaces it with fresher, drier air.

## Cutting down on energy

Most modern electrical and gas appliances are far more energy-efficient than in the past. Many now have some form of energy efficiency logo or badge. In the European Union, this is a rating from A (the most efficient) to G. In Asia and the Pacific (for example, Japan, Indonesia, and the Philippines), about three-quarters of countries have some form of energy-efficiency labeling. In the U.S., most stores and suppliers display an Energy Guide, allowing buyers to compare the energy-efficiency of all of the appliances on sale. In other countries, particularly in the southern hemisphere, appliances such as refrigerators have been developed that are powered by biogas or by photovoltaic cells that use energy from the sun.

## Nothing new

Passive ventilation in homes makes use of simple design features and involves no moving parts at all. Vertical ducts or pipes run from the kitchen and bathroom to vents (openings) in the roof, drawing moist air out of the building. Traditional methods of passive ventilation have been used in desert countries for thousands of years. These make use of the large variations in temperature between day and night and in different parts of the building. They depend on air being drawn from cooler parts of the building as warmer air is allowed to escape.

These homes in Croydon, Britain, are part of an eco-friendly housing estate. These homes make use of passive ventilation through the ducts on top of the roofs.

More expensive, energy-efficient light bulbs (compact fluorescent lights, or CFLs) can save up to 10 times the cost of ordinary bulbs over their lifetime, besides saving electricity. Because of their low energy requirements, CFLs are also ideal for using with photovoltaic cells. Further savings can be achieved with automatic light sensors in communal areas, such as hallways or courtyards in apartment buildings, which means lights are not left on needlessly.

Insulating walls by filling wall cavities (the space between the inner and outer wall) with various types of insulating material can reduce heat loss by more than 40 percent. Attic insulation can reduce heat loss by 20 percent, while carpets can reduce heat loss through floors by 60 percent. Some types of insulating materials can be responsible for generating toxic by-products, however, during both their manufacture and use. Double or triple glazing will cut down heat loss through windows but can be expensive. Like some forms of insulation, manufacturing the frames—usually from a material called PVC—can also produce harmful by-products.

## What color is your electricity?

In many countries, it is now possible to switch the electricity supply to one known as "green power." This means that the supplier has to match the energy used with electricity produced from a renewable source, such as wind or biomass. In the U.S., more than 50 percent of households have an option to purchase some form of green power, although not all do. All U.S. consumers can also purchase "renewable energy certificates." This means some of the money from their energy bills supports sustainable energy projects elsewhere in the world.

Putting insulation in the attic of your home reduces heat loss and therefore saves energy.

Poorly designed and inefficient wood-burning stoves damage health and the environment in both developing and developed countries.

## Energy kills?

Perhaps surprisingly, one of the biggest killers in many developing countries is the wood-burning stove. The inefficient way these stoves burn produces smoke particles that enter and damage the lungs. Poisonous gases, such as carbon monoxide, and cancer-causing chemicals, such as dioxins, are also produced. Worldwide, up to two billion people may be exposed to higher risks of lung disease in this way.

Damage to health caused by burning wood is not only an issue for poor countries. It is estimated that there are 11 million wood-burning stoves in the U.S., burning 47 million tons (43 million t) of wood each year. Burning two pounds (1 kg) of wood, even in a modern wood stove, releases into the atmosphere four and a half ounces (130 g) of carbon monoxide and a third of an ounce (10 g) of cancer-causing benzene. A typical U.S. wood-burning stove is several thousand times "dirtier" than burning natural gas.

## Case Study: Making a better stove

Energy-efficient stoves are designed so that the wood or animal dung burns at a higher temperature, so fewer toxic products are produced. They also burn less fuel, so less wood is used. In the case of dung, this means that more can be left available to use as fertilizer rather than fuel. There are many other ways of increasing the efficiency of stoves, such as adding a chimney to increase the flow of air over the fire. A "pot skirt" that channels hot air against the bottom and sides of the pot also helps to increase efficiency. Even more effective, however, is to have part of the pot set into the stove itself. Recent cooking stove designs in India encourage the use of family cooking pots as a template when constructing new stoves. This means the pot fits snugly against the heat source.

This twin-pot wood-burning stove uses fuel more efficiently than traditional stoves. It allows one pot to heat rapidly while the other is left simmering.

# Living with less water

You might not think so, but water is a scarce resource. Most parts of the world experience water shortages at some time during the year. As the global climate changes and becomes more unpredictable, the availability of water is likely to become an increasingly pressing problem for most homes, wherever they are.

## Water use

This is not just a question of water availability. Supplying homes with water and, just as importantly, treating the dirty water we produce, uses energy—about 220 kilowatt-hours for an average European household every year. That's enough to boil a kettle for 100 hours!

In the developed world, we are using more and more water in our homes. In the UK, for example, water consumption has risen by more than 70 percent in the last 30 years. North America's largest aquifer (underground water supply), the Ogallala, is being used up at the rate of 424 billion cubic feet (12 billion cu m) a year. Agriculture and increasing demand from cities accounts for much of this. In developing parts of the world, increasing water use is also a problem. In cities, increasing numbers of better-off families are demanding better standards of living, including improved water supplies. In rural areas, growing cash crops, such as coffee, for export to richer countries puts still more pressure on scarce groundwater supplies. Often, these crops require more water than traditional crops.

Water treatment plants, such as this one in Colorado, process water so that it is safe for drinking. This processing uses up huge amounts of energy.

It is easy to take water for granted. After all, for many of us, water is just something that comes out of the faucet whenever we want it. In poorer parts of the world, people take very little for granted, particularly water, and especially clean water. Waterborne diseases, caused by unclean and untreated water, are still major killers in many parts of the world. Cholera alone affects 5.5 million people, causing 120,000 deaths each year. Waterborne diseases indirectly fill half of the developing world's hospital beds.

## Water, water everywhere?

The table and pie chart below show the daily and yearly water consumption in a typical home in the developed world—per person. For comparison, people in developed countries use about 10 times as much water as those in poor countries, while two-fifths of the world's population faces serious water shortages.

| Water use | Daily amount gallons (liters) | Annual amount gallons |
|---|---|---|
| Kitchen | 6.3 (24) | 2,314 (8,760) |
| Washing clothes | 8.5 (32) | 3,086 (11,680) |
| Dishwasher | 0.4 (1.6) | 154 (584) |
| Toilet flushing | 13.1 (49.6) | 4,783 (18,104) |
| Garden | 1.7 (6.4) | 617 (2,336) |
| Bath | 6.3 (24) | 2,314 (8,760) |
| Shower | 2.1 (8) | 771 (2,920) |
| Personal washing (in addition to baths and showers) | 3.8 (14.4) | 1,124 (4,256) |
| Total | 42.2 (160) | 15,163 (57,400) |

- Toilet flushing
- Kitchen
- Personal washing
- Garden
- Washing clothes
- Bath
- Shower
- Dishwasher

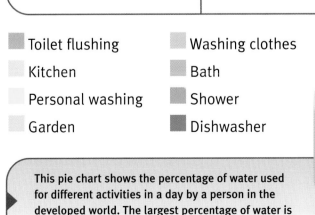

20%
31%
15%
15%
9%
5%
4%
1%

This pie chart shows the percentage of water used for different activities in a day by a person in the developed world. The largest percentage of water is used to flush the toilet!

Source: Southern Water, 2002.

## Flushing water away

People in developed countries use most water to flush the toilet. In the UK, homes built before about 1990 (where the toilet has not been replaced) use two and a third gallons (9 L) of water with every flush. More modern, dual-flush toilets have two options: a long and a short flush. In addition, low-flush models or placing bricks in the tank, which take up some of the space normally occupied by water, can help reduce water use by up to 20 percent.

> Taking a shower instead of a bath saves water and energy. If you have an energy-efficient showerhead, you can save even more water.

## Washing water away

The average bath uses about 21 gallons (80 L) of water. Shorter or shallower bathtubs can be a form of passive water saving. Obviously, though, not filling the bathtub with water is a simple alternative! Showering, on average, uses less than half as much water as a bath, and water-efficient showerheads reduce the amount of water still more. Devices called aerators can be attached to faucets in sinks to reduce their flow without making them less effective. Spray faucets also cut down water use, but in hard-water areas, they tend to get blocked with scale and have to be treated regularly.

# Case Study: Two views of saving water

Watton Green is a development of 11 houses in Birmingham, Britain. The installation of one-and-a-half-gallon (6 L) toilets, aerated faucets, shallow baths, and a garden rain barrel helped reduce water use to around 26 gallons (100 L) per person per day. This resulted in a savings of around 16 gallons (60 L) of water each day.

Before the water industry was privatized in South Africa, many poor families were denied access to adequate water supplies. Now, families receive 1,585 gallons (6,000 L) of water a month for free. This means 13 gallons (50 L) a day for a family of 4 people. Above this amount, they pay. The United Nations says that 13 gallons (50 L) a day is the basic domestic water requirement. Of course, not every South African family has only four members. Does this sound like a fair system?

## Water for crops

In poor or dry countries, up to 80 percent of water goes to irrigating crops. In many Indian villages, drinking water supplies from traditional wells and boreholes have been badly affected by overextraction of groundwater for crops. Methods such as drip irrigation, which uses perforated pipes to water plants precisely, reduce waste, as do low-pressure sprinklers. Building small wall dams slows down the rate of runoff of rainfall and allows it more time to soak into the groundwater. This replenishes drinking water sources for small communities in rural areas.

In the dusty farming district of Makueni, Kenya, families draw drinking water from this well in a dry riverbed. The small water supply in this area is shared between domestic use and farming. In order for crops to survive, farmers must pump the water to use for irrigation—meaning there is less water for drinking.

## Too clean?

Treating wastewater is expensive and uses large amounts of energy. The water most of us get from our faucets is purified to a very high level to make it suitable for drinking. There are systems that recycle water used for washing or showering and then treat it to a lower standard than drinking water. The recycled water is then made available again for "nonpersonal" use, such as flushing the toilet or gardening. This kind of system is known as a gray-water system. It saves energy and water but is easier to install in residential accommodations such as apartments than in individual houses. Not everyone likes the idea, though, because some people think it is "dirty" water. The water isn't really dirty, but it may contain higher levels of certain chemicals, depending, for example, on what cleaning products have been used. It is not suitable for drinking, but it is fine for flushing the toilet!

## Bringing in the rain

Of course, recycling or collecting water is nothing new. Most of us are familiar with the idea of an outside rain barrel that collects rainwater from the roof. Wash water can also be emptied onto plants rather than down the drain. In many countries where water is permanently in short supply or contaminated by contact with human or animal waste, collecting rainwater is vital to survival.

Water shortage is not just a problem in hot countries in the developing world. In the developed world, too, we need to think about recycling water in our homes and gardens whenever possible.

HERR MEMORIAL LIBRARY

In much of the world, particularly Asia and Africa, the collection and storage of rainwater still serves as a major source of drinking water in rural areas. Reasonably pure rainwater can be collected from roofs constructed with galvanized corrugated iron, aluminum, or cement sheets, tiles, slates, and even thatch. It is important to keep the roofs clean and free from bird droppings, and to have good-quality storage vessels. Simple filters, such as fine cotton cloth, can also be used to remove any particles of dirt.

## Case study: Water crisis in Lebanon

In Lebanon, natural water scarcity, increased demand, and poor wastewater treatment are leading to a water crisis. Often, wastewater is released untreated or captured in septic tanks, which may leak, causing contamination of groundwater. Several towns in West Bekaa are testing a gray-water system for recycling the wastewater, using what are known as trickle filters. The goal is to use the recycled water for urban horticulture, increasing the availability of fresh food and generating income while safeguarding freshwater supplies. High levels of community involvement are important if the idea is to be successful and introduced more widely in the country.

This rainwater collection system in Belize catches water that falls on the roofs of nearby huts in a tank. The water has not been contaminated by contact with human or animal waste and is reasonably pure as long as the roofs are kept clean.

## Treating wastewater

In most developed countries, modern wastewater treatment plants are very efficient, but the treatment is expensive and also uses a great deal of water. There are more sustainable ways of treating our own waste, depending on location, although they will not always be appropriate or even possible.

## Reed bed system

Reed beds are natural water purifiers. Certain types of reed have the ability to absorb oxygen from the air and release it through their roots. This creates ideal conditions for the development of huge numbers of microorganisms, which are able to break down human or other waste.

In a typical reed bed system, sewage and other wastewater is collected in underground tanks. The liquid is pumped into a "filtering stack," where it trickles down through stone chippings before entering a planted reed bed. This is a large tank of reeds planted on graded gravel topped with sand. From here, the treated liquid enters a lake via a marshy area. By now, it is free of any harmful organisms such as bacteria. The remaining solids settle for a while and are then pumped out to a "sludge bed," which is planted with another type of reed. The solids are allowed to form compost and are then dug out every 10 years for use as fertilizer.

Nile cabbage in this pond in Baobab, Mombasa, removes any excess impurities and nutrients from the water in which it grows. Once purified, the water is reused by a nearby fish farm.

## A big PR problem?

Perhaps for obvious reasons, dry toilets are not popular. In Mexico, modern (water-based) sanitation is undermining the stability of the soil as more and more groundwater is pumped out to meet demand. A flushing toilet is a status symbol, since it is a visible sign of wealth. Education and pointing out the advantages of dry systems—which include lower costs—take time and are not always successful. How would you "sell" the idea of dry toilets to a doubtful family? How would you feel about having one installed in your home?

A reed bed system must suit the circumstances and landscape of a particular site, and not all designs are the same. In India, lilies are grown in the water, rather than reeds. In parts of South America, Asia, and Africa, waste stabilization ponds are widely used. These are shallow lakes in which treatment of wastewater occurs through the natural biological activities of algae and bacteria.

### Dry toilets

Dry or composting toilets go one step further. They don't use water at all. Basically, they consist of two vaults: one in use, and the other composting. In the vault that is in use, the waste material is constantly covered with lime or ash. These dry toilets can be installed inside or outside the house and are inexpensive to build. Designed properly, they don't smell, and the waste is a valuable source of fertilizer.

Dry toilets can dispose of sewage just as effectively as flush toilets, without wasting valuable water.

### A good compromise?

In parts of rural India and China, a compromise solution to the dry toilet is a "pour-flush" twin-pit toilet, which uses the minimum amount of water to clean the small toilet pan. This water is usually household wastewater. This kind of toilet is more popular than a dry toilet and also saves the ash or lime, which can be used to improve soil instead. As with this example, living in a sustainable home may sometimes mean striking a balance between an ideal solution and a practical one.

27

# Reducing waste and cutting pollution

On average, a person living in Europe produces about half a ton (.5 t) of household waste or garbage each year. In the U.S., the average is four-fifths of a ton (.75 t) per person. In order to make our homes more sustainable, we must reduce the amount of unnecessary waste we produce.

In both Europe and the U.S., most waste (57 percent) ends up in landfills, and many regions are now running out of places to bury it. Landfills generate methane, which is a powerful greenhouse gas, as the garbage decomposes. Although this is sometimes piped off for use as a fuel, in the form of biogas, most of it escapes. In Europe, a further 19 percent (14 percent in the U.S.) of waste is burned in incinerators. This can also be a valuable source of energy, but few people want waste incinerators near their homes.

## Reduce: use less, gain more

Since more than 25 percent of garbage can waste is packaging, avoiding overpackaged goods is a good way to reduce waste. Removing your address from mailing lists can reduce the amount of junk mail and free newspapers you receive. This can be quite complicated, however, and different countries operate different systems. In the U.S., four and a half million tons (4 million t) of junk mail are sent out every year, and 50 percent of it is never even opened.

Burning garbage in incinerators is one way of dealing with garbage, but it would be far better for the environment if we produced less garbage in the first place. The emissions from this chimney are contributing to global warming and may contain toxic products.

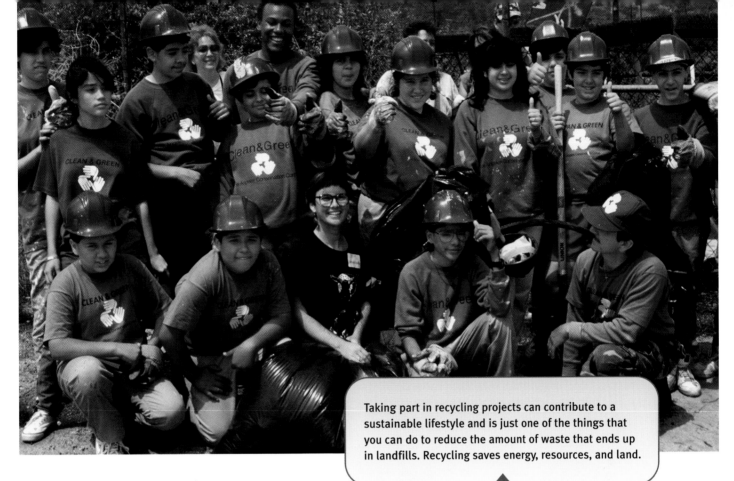

Taking part in recycling projects can contribute to a sustainable lifestyle and is just one of the things that you can do to reduce the amount of waste that ends up in landfills. Recycling saves energy, resources, and land.

## Reuse again and again

Reusing items such as grocery bags and using waste paper for scrap are obvious examples of ways we can reuse items. Thrift shops are also great at recycling goods. In poorer countries, very few items are ever thrown away because they are seen as valuable resources that can be used for other purposes. Oil cans become sheet metal statues or model cars, and plastic containers become water carriers.

Here is a small challenge—before throwing something away, think if there is another use for it, or before buying a new item, check if there is something already in your home that you could use instead.

## Recycle: don't just throw it away

All developed countries have some system that provides local services such as garbage collection, recreational facilities, or social services. Most of these authorities also run recycling programs. Often, they are doorstep or curbside collections for items such as paper, plastic, glass, aluminum, and steel cans. The U.S., which recycles 31 percent of its domestic waste, now has more than 9,000 curbside collections, as well as 12,000 "drop-off" centers for recyclable material. Some authorities provide recycling facilities for textiles and garden waste, which could also be composted at home.

*"If you do your recycling of your newspapers, you're saving on the cutting down of trees—recycling keeps garbage from being dumped on the countryside."*

Retiree

*"Actually, I can't see the point [of recycling]; I don't produce enough garbage to make a difference, and, anyway, the time needed to sort it is just not worth the trouble."*

Person moving into apartments run in a sustainable way

## Recycling in developing countries

In many rapidly developing countries, recycling takes place by individuals as a matter of necessity—and sometimes survival. Large urban garbage dumps in countries such as Brazil support whole communities that scavenge for reusable or recyclable materials, often at great risk to themselves. This does not mean that organized recycling does not happen. Many South American countries, including Brazil, Argentina, and Uruguay, have passed what are known as Extended Producer Responsibility (EPR) laws. This means that manufacturers of certain products, such as batteries, lamps, and printer cartridges, must provide facilities to take them back once they are used so that they can be recycled or disposed of safely.

## Recycling in the developed world

Most homeowners are willing to go to a bit of extra trouble to separate their garbage, but in many countries, more encouragement and better recycling facilities could increase recycling rates dramatically. In Switzerland, it is an offense not to separate garbage. In Germany, people are charged by how much they throw away. Look at the recycling records for Switzerland and Germany in the bar chart (below). Do you think the laws about recycling in these countries are a good idea, or should people be allowed to make up their own minds?

The "Castle," in New Mexico, is a home made of beer cans and mud. It is the first of several sustainable buildings designed to show what can be achieved using waste materials and sustainable methods.

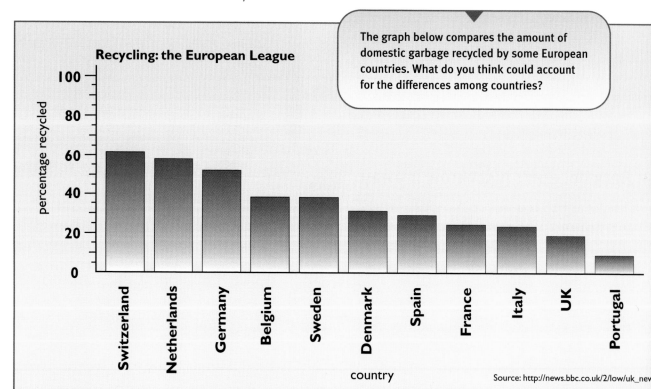

### Recycling: the European League

The graph below compares the amount of domestic garbage recycled by some European countries. What do you think could account for the differences among countries?

*percentage recycled*

100
80
60
40
20
0

Switzerland · Netherlands · Germany · Belgium · Sweden · Denmark · Spain · France · Italy · UK · Portugal

country

Source: http://news.bbc.co.uk/2/low/uk_new

## Using better household materials

In addition to generating waste, our homes can also be a source of harmful or toxic substances. Some of these may be responsible for the large increases in asthma and other allergic reactions experienced by people in many parts of the world. Some substances may even cause cancer. Others can cause direct damage to the environment and to wildlife.

In countries that can obtain wood grown from sustainable resources, timber window frames are preferable to frames made from

PVC, which is a type of plastic. The manufacture of PVC involves the use of oil (itself a nonrenewable resource) and also releases toxic chemicals called dioxins. Natural paints, varnishes, and some types of glue give off fewer harmful fumes than oil-based products. Insulation can be made out of cellulose (obtained from wood or recycled paper) rather than materials made from oil or minerals.

Homes made with timber frames are environmentally friendly as long as the timber comes from a sustainably managed forest where new trees are planted as mature trees are cut down.

## Hurting the poor

In countries where wood is scarce, harmful building materials are frequently used because they are cheap. Asbestos sheeting is sometimes dumped on poorer countries by richer nations, where its use is now banned because dust from asbestos is highly carcinogenic, or cancer-inducing. A far better alternative is ferro-cement, which uses a minimum of cement mix, reinforced with wire mesh, to produce a lightweight, cost-effective building material. Roof sections, beams and posts, doors, window frames, rafters, and composting toilets can be made using this technology. In India, ferro-cement is also used widely for constructing tanks for collecting rainwater.

## Killer in the cupboard?

Bleach-based cleaning products and disinfectants, designed to kill germs, can harm the microorganisms that break down waste material in water treatment plants. Perhaps more alarming are the many new and complex chemicals found in products such as stain removers, flame retardants, food packaging, floor polishes, household lubricants, and even children's toys (see page 33).

We can't always avoid using products such as these in the home, but we can be more aware of the possible dangers they pose. In Europe, products meeting high environmental standards have a distinctive eco-label. Plastics with the numbers three or seven inside the recycling logo are likely to contain harmful substances called phthalates. In the U.S., of the 62,000 chemicals on the market, only a tiny percentage have been tested for long-term toxic effects. Although the U.S. Food and Drug Administration requires comprehensive labeling of products, it is easy to hide potentially toxic chemicals under trade or other names.

The issue of household chemicals is complex because not all of the scientific research is completely proven. In the end, it is probably sensible to be sparing when using any manufactured household product and to try to use more natural or organic alternatives whenever possible.

Many of the cleaning products we are familiar with in our homes are more dangerous than we think.

# Chemicals on the danger list

Many chemicals found in modern products remain in the environment for a long time. They can build up in our bodies and in those of wild animals. This is especially true in the case of top predators, such as seals or birds of prey. The chemicals pass up the food chain and become more concentrated. Substances called phthalates, used as plastic softeners, are known as hormone disrupters. They block the normal action of hormones, especially sex hormones. This may lead to conditions such as testicular cancer. Chemicals called phenols, used in computer cases, crash helmets, and the plastic lining of food cans, have been shown to have a "feminizing" effect on mollusks, fish, and birds, although their effects on humans are not known.

Common seals are at great risk from pollution caused by chemicals from household waste. Since they are top predators, toxic chemicals build up in the food chain and become concentrated in animals such as this.

# CHAPTER 5

# Positive action

In addition to thinking about the negative impact of our homes on the environment, we need to look at the idea of sustainable homes as having a positive effect. Good designs that fit in with the local surroundings will enhance the environment. Using local materials and skills, thereby creating local jobs, also has a positive effect. Buying locally grown food cuts down on transportation bills and fuel and supports local farmers. For those with gardens, growing vegetables also makes homes more sustainable. At the same time, waste plant material can be used to make compost, which reduces the need for artificial fertilizers.

## Growing organic food

Organically grown food has had no chemical fertilizers or pesticides used on it at all. There is general agreement that this is better for the environment because pesticides kill beneficial organisms as well as ones that damage crops. Organic food may also be better for our health. It is, however, more expensive than conventionally grown products. The benefits to the environment may well be worth this additional cost. These benefits include stopping the long-term damage done to soil structure by the continuous use of chemical fertilizers.

Growing your own vegetables can make your home more sustainable. It is important to make sure, however, that the soil has not been contaminated by past industrial use.

A crew of foresters in Costa Rica plants trees in the Puriscal region for the environmental group Arbofilia. This project brings farmers and nursery workers together to reforest the land and manage it sustainably.

It is also important to think about organic produce when buying food from overseas, particularly from developing countries. Unless the food is organically grown, poor farmers are often exposed to high levels of toxic chemicals, with little protection or knowledge of the health risks they face. Buying food from poorer countries with some kind of "fair trade" labeling means that the original growers have received a reasonable price for their produce and are not being exploited. This, in turn, reduces poverty. This is important in itself, but more so because poor people are often forced to damage their environment in order to obtain the resources they need. Reducing poverty can also benefit the environment by preventing the need for this damage.

## Better buildings

The building materials we use can also have a positive effect. Timber frame construction using timber grown from a sustainable source means that mature trees, which have finished growing and are carbon neutral, are replaced by saplings, which are growing rapidly and therefore absorb more carbon dioxide. Labeling of sustainably grown timber is now covered by various internationally recognized programs—principally, the Forestry Stewardship Council (FSC) program and the Pan-European Forest Certification program.

Timber is an excellent building material that keeps buildings cool in the summer and reduces heating costs in the winter. The use of toxic glues can be reduced by using the wood's natural lignin instead. In one construction system, preformed timber panels are built with cellulose fiber insulation already sandwiched between the panels. This reduces waste and means that the panels have what is known as low embodied energy. This means that as little energy as possible goes into their construction and transport.

35

Providing food for birds is just one way of supporting your local wildlife and making your home more sustainable. Make sure the food is fresh and any nuts are unsalted. Birds in the garden are also beneficial because they help to control insect pests. If you start feeding birds in your garden, remember that you must feed them year-round—not just in the winter.

## Learning to live with wildlife

We tend to think of human habitation as being damaging to wildlife or the habitats where wild animals and plants live, and often it is. But in most homes, there is likely to be some kind of open space nearby, whether it is in the form of a garden, yard, green space, communal area, or just a window box. The way this space is managed—for example, the types of plants grown there—can greatly benefit local wildlife. Similarly, the avoidance of garden chemicals, such as slug killers or pesticides (for which there are many natural alternatives), will also have a positive impact on wildlife. In fact, killing garden pests can often do more harm than good because beneficial species may also be eliminated.

## Supporting your local wildlife

You can support your local wildlife by:

- providing food for birds, such as nuts (not salted), fat, and sunflower seeds

- putting out water for birds to drink and possibly bathe in
- putting up nesting boxes; keeping them out of direct sunlight and out of reach of predators
- adding compost or rotting leaves to soil to make it richer and to improve the habitat for small insects (and to benefit the larger animals, such as hedgehogs, frogs, and birds, that feed on them)
- sprinkling wildflower seeds in a suitable corner; once grown, these will attract butterflies and other insects
- if space allows, building a small pond to benefit frogs and dragonflies; add a small plank or large stones so animals can get out
- creating dark, damp corners for amphibians such as frogs, toads, and newts
- planting "cover" such as hedges or shrubs; this will encourage insects and songbirds.

## Location, location

Ideally, new sustainable homes should be built on what are called brownfield sites. These are sites on which previous housing or industrial premises have existed. This is not always possible, or even desirable, however. In some cases, industrial land is polluted with toxic chemicals such as lead and cadmium. Removing polluted soil is costly and can expose workers to health hazards. When greenfield sites—sites that have not previously been built on—are chosen, care needs to be taken to avoid land that is ecologically important. However, brownfield sites may also develop interesting or rare wildlife over time, and these, too, need to be protected.

## Case Study: Building homes for people and nature

Loudoun County eco-village is situated on a third of a square mile (.7 sq km) of organically managed land in Virginia. The village follows the natural contours of the land, and biodiversity (the variety of living things) is maintained by careful land planning and planting. Construction practices preserve existing forest, soil, and water. Landscaping is based on native plants, ground cover, and wildflowers. Cars are excluded from the center of the village, and there are many pedestrian trails allowing residents to move around the village and enjoy its natural features.

*"Living here has given me a feeling of connection to nature and our neighbors; I have found a neighborhood that reflects my values."*

Resident

These homes have been built on a greenfield site in the UK. Although greenfield sites offer a nice environment for people to live in, it is important that housing does not destroy areas of environmental importance—this is not sustainable development.

# Building sustainable communities

Perhaps the most important factor that makes a home a good place to live is the community—the people who live there. But what do we really mean by sustainable communities? They are places where people work together to create a fairer, more sustainable way of doing things. Rather than working individually, they share resources and ideas to produce a better quality of life for everyone.

## Better homes for people

In most countries, both rich and poor, many people find it hard to find good-quality, affordable housing in the places they want to live and work. Sustainable communities are attempts to combine these ideas in a way that does not make unsustainable demands on resources. Often, they are partnerships among local authorities, local businesses, and voluntary organizations that share the same vision of a more sustainable future.

> "Creating sustainable communities means putting sustainable development into practice. Sustainable communities must combine social inclusion [involving people], homes, jobs, services, infrastructure [local services and transportation], and respect for the environment to create places where people will want to live and work now and in the future."
>
> John Prescott, UK Deputy Prime Minister

Carefully planned and well-designed housing can provide people with a better quality of life. In previously run-down areas, new developments like this one have shown an improvement in people's well-being and have encouraged residents to take better care of their homes and the environment.

Communities such as this one in San Jose, California, share common ideas about the environment they want to live in. This can lead to less vandalism and people looking after their surroundings by not dropping litter.

This is not just a question of reducing energy use or cutting down waste. It is about building communities that work better in a more general sense. They are sometimes described as being "socially inclusive." This means that everyone, whatever their beliefs, ethnic origin, or background, feels like part of a community where different views are tolerated and valued and responsibilities are shared. The homes themselves should be well designed and well built and, as far as possible, fit in with the local environment. They should have good transportation services and other forms of communication linking people to jobs, schools, health services, recreational facilities, stores, and other services. They should also be fair: everyone, no matter what their situations, should benefit equally from

the services and resources available. Finally, of course, they should be environmentally sensitive, providing places for people to live that take account of the needs of the environment.

Communities that work together and share common ideas and goals tend to work better than those that do not. There are often other benefits, too, such as lower crime rates, less vandalism, better individual health, and more "social interaction." In short, people have more say in what goes on in their community and therefore value it more highly.

39

## Getting the infrastructure right

Sustainable communities are not about building sustainable homes in isolation. Of equal importance are the many services, such as stores and other facilities, needed to support that community—the infrastructure. Unless the right services are available, in the right places, and within reach of the people who need them, many of the benefits of sustainable housing will be lost.

## Transportation and communication

Transportation and communication are crucial when developing sustainable communities. Look at the example in the box (right). Make a list of the different services and other features mentioned and their distance from the community. How do you think these features contribute to making this community more sustainable? Many of the developments are designed to reduce car use. This will reduce the overall energy consumption of the community and cut down pollution. To achieve this, the provision of efficient and affordable public transportation, such as trains and buses, within easy reach of the community is essential.

## A question of communications

A housing group in Firgrove, Britain, developed a small group of two-bedroom houses. The houses are 1,640 feet (500 m) from a bus stop with routes to several towns and the railway station. A mailbox and grocery store are also within 1,640 feet (500 m) of the houses. A post office, pharmacy, school, medical center, community center, and bar are all within a mile (1.6 km). A sidewalk connects the site to the bus stop. Space is available in one of the bedrooms in each house for a home office. Secure bike storage is also provided.

If everyone in a community used public transportation instead of cars for short journeys, an enormous amount of fuel could be saved. This would also mean fewer emissions and a healthier environment. Public transportation must be clean and reliable, like this modern streetcar in Strasbourg, France, if people are going to be encouraged to use it.

# Case Study: LA eco-village

Los Angeles eco-village in California is only one block (a few hundred feet) east of one of the city's busiest traffic corridors. It is part of a 2-block neighborhood consisting of 48 housing units. The buildings are gradually being refurbished to reduce their environmental impact. In addition, there is a demonstration gray-water system (see page 24), an electric vehicle sharing program, and the cooperative buying of organic food and environmentally safe household products.

Perhaps just as important as these features, however, is the thinking behind the project. The idea is to demonstrate how a diverse, or mixed, population can live more sustainably in an urban environment, as one of the residents describes:

"We try to figure out how the problems in our neighborhood are related to the problems in the wider environment. We are especially interested in how these problems relate to our ability to have healthy air, water, and soil, human health, a decent standard of living, a high quality of life, nonpolluting livelihood, and a strong sense of community. Through working together with our own skills and resources, we begin to create changes in our neighborhood at the pace we can incorporate them into our lives physically, socially, and economically. There is much opportunity for collaboration and building consensus [agreement]."

More and more people are choosing to work from a home office. Home working can contribute toward a more sustainable way of living by reducing the need for travel.

## The United Nations Climate Change Conference

Former U.S. president Bill Clinton (left) and Canadian prime minister Paul Martin played a big part in the 2005 United Nations Conference on Climate Change in Montreal, Canada. In a speech, Clinton said that cutting greenhouse gases was good for business and the planet.

## Using the power of government

Most governments now recognize the connection between sustainable communities and healthy societies. They have also become concerned about the impact of human activity on the environment. In particular, the effects of global warming have forced governments and other bodies, especially those in developed countries, to bring in tough new standards for constructing homes and other buildings that are designed to reduce energy use.

In Europe, the "Energy Performance of Buildings Directive" requires all member states to set minimum standards of energy-efficiency on all new buildings, as well as on large buildings undergoing major renovation. In a typical European country, the goal is to improve energy-efficiency in domestic homes by an average of 20 percent by 2010. It is calculated that energy standards of new homes will deliver a reduction in carbon emissions of one and a half million tons (1.4 million t) a year.

Many of these regulations go far beyond the use of energy. Increasingly, governments are developing standards for the efficient use of resources in general, including those relating to water, transportation, and waste.

*"In years to come, this is what we've got to use: low-energy lights. That's all there is to it."*

**Resident living in environmental apartment**

*"The [low-energy] lights are so cheap to run, you can use as much as you like. So I leave all the lights on."*

**Retiree**

## Not for everyone?

Not everyone will share the same views about sustainable communities or want to be involved. This is particularly true when people move into the community without understanding or being part of the vision that created the community in the first place. For example, some people prefer to use ordinary light bulbs, rather than feeling they have to use low-energy ones. Or, because low-energy bulbs cost less to run, they feel they can use them more. Saving waste, such as paper or plastic, may also be seen in very different ways.

Other people may be prepared to act in ways that are more sustainable when it saves them money or time, but not when there is inconvenience or no savings to themselves. For example, providing good public transportation systems does not necessarily mean people will use them if it is more convenient to take the car. Look at the views on this page. What do you think about these issues? People need to be convinced of the benefits before they will participate fully, and even when the benefits are clear, it takes time to build new communities.

> *"I guess it's the guilt, isn't it? You live in an environmentally friendly house, so you feel like you ought to do it [recycle]."*
>
> Resident of environmentally friendly housing

> *"In wintertime, you're in and out in all weather to put a couple of bits of plastic in one bin and a bit of newspaper in another. So it doesn't really make it easy for you."*
>
> New resident to environmentally friendly housing

New houses have to be built with energy-saving and other sustainable measures in mind. Housing will only continue to become more sustainable through a mixture of government regulation and action by individuals.

43

# No place like a sustainable home

There are many different kinds of sustainable homes and many different approaches to living in a sustainable community. It may involve an eco-village where everything is designed to minimize the impact on the environment. It may be a small group of new homes built to high environmental standards. It may be an old housing project or city block that is gradually renovated to be more energy-efficient. It may be in a poor rural area or in a city anywhere in the world.

For each of these different approaches to sustainable living, different solutions are needed. Some of these will require governments and planners to act; others will require investment in new technologies by industry and other bodies; some will require communities themselves to take control.

This home is built into a hillside. It is extremely eco-friendly and a great example of sustainable living. The glass windows let in heat and light, and this heat is retained well by the surrounding hillside.

We all live in different types of houses. Many of us do not live in specially built eco-homes or eco-villages, but that does not mean that we cannot take action for sustainability. A few simple changes to your lifestyle can make a big difference.

## What about us?

While it may be easier to plan and build new, sustainable homes, the reality is that most of us will continue to live in ordinary, existing homes in ordinary towns, cities, and villages. But that does not mean we can't make those homes and communities more sustainable. You could, of course, ask, "Why bother?" Most people now recognize that the majority of us—whether in rich or poor countries, and for different reasons—are living in ways that are unsustainable. We are damaging the environment and, in the process, harming ourselves as well. Unless we somehow change the way we live, the consequences may be serious for us all.

It is sometimes difficult to feel that you have any influence over these issues. However, change is always possible, particularly if you feel it is important enough. For example, you could look at the way you travel to school or other locations. You may have already done this.

Many schools now encourage more sustainable ways of traveling to and from the site. How could this be promoted more effectively? Youth groups and clubs are also good places to look for ways of doing things more sustainably. If you have access to the Internet, try typing in the name of your state and the words "sustainable communities." See what you find! The local library should also have plenty of information. Finally, you can also change what you do in your home itself.

## Your choice

Living more sustainably is a matter of choice. After all, why should you change the way you live if others are not prepared to do the same? Sustainable homes are not just fine ideas for those who can afford them; they are at the heart of successful and healthy communities worldwide. In the end, it is your community—and your choice.

# Glossary

**asbestos** a highly heat-resistant substance used in fire-resistant and insulating materials; asbestos particles can cause cancer if inhaled

**biogas** the name given to the mix of gases produced by rotting organic matter; biogas can be used as a fuel

**biomass** organic matter used as a fuel; biomass is often used to generate electricity

**borehole** a deep, narrow hole in the ground that is drilled to find water

**carcinogen** a substance that can cause cancer

**combined heat and power (CHP)** efficient technology in which the heat produced during the generation of electricity is recovered and used

**deforestation** the clearing of trees from an area

**developed countries** the richer, industrialized countries of the world, including the U.S., Australia, Japan, and European countries

**developing countries** the poorer countries of the world, such as some African, Asian, and South American countries, which are working to develop

**dioxin** an extremely toxic substance that is produced as a by-product of some manufacturing processes

**ecology** relation of organisms to one another and to their physical surroundings

**fair trade** trade that involves developing world farmers being paid a fair price for their produce

**fermenter** a container in which organic material is broken down by natural processes to produce either methane gas or alcohol, either of which can be used as fuel

**ferro-cement** a strong, lightweight building material with less cement than normal concrete

**fossil fuel** a substance, such as coal, oil, or gas, that is formed from the decomposition of animal and plant remains; fossil fuels release carbon dioxide when they are burned

**greenhouse gas** a gas, such as carbon dioxide, that contributes to global warming and climate change

**groundwater** water from underground sources

**incinerator** a place where waste can be burned

**irrigation** supplying water to farmland, usually by a system of canals and pipes

**lignin** a substance found in the cell walls of many plants and trees

**microclimate** the climate of a small area such as a forest or even inside a building

**organic** derived from living organisms

**photovoltaic cells** devices that are used to produce electricity using direct sunlight

**PV array** a group of photovoltaic cells

**raw material** the basic material from which a product is made; oil is one of the raw materials of plastic

**refurbish** to repair something to bring it back into good working order; a refurbished house is one that has been made fit to live in

**resources** assets or materials that are valuable; the world's natural resources include water and fossil fuels such as coal, gas, and oil

**slurry** runny mixture usually made of manure, cement, or coal, and water

**toxic** poisonous

# Further information

## Web sites

### Ecovillage Findhorn

http://www.ecovillagefindhorn.com
Web site for the Findhorn Foundation, based in Scotland. The goal is to create linked "eco-villages" around the world through the Global Ecovillage Network.

### Friends of the Earth

http://www.foe.org
Web site of Friends of the Earth. Produces information and educational material on all aspects of sustainability and the environment, particularly reducing pollution and waste.

### The Sustainable Homes Initiative

http://www.sustainablehomes.org
Web site run by the International Institute for Energy Conservation. Gives examples of sustainable communities worldwide, particularly in Africa, and includes an A–Z of eco-technologies.

### WWF: One Planet Living Communities

http://www.panda.org/about_wwf/what_we_do/
policy/one_planet_living/communities/
index.cfm
Information about the Worldwide Fund for Nature program aimed at creating zero carbon, zero waste communities.

### EcoVillage at Ithaca

http://www.ecovillage.ithaca.ny.us/default.html
Web site of an eco-village in Ithaca, New York. Includes a virtual tour.

### Context Institute

http://www.context.org/index.html
Home page of the Context Institute, a nonprofit organization that explores what is necessary in the development of "humane sustainable culture."

### Smart Communities Network

http://www.smartcommunities.ncat.org/
The Smart Communities Network offers information about "green development," community energy, and land use.

### Energy Savers

http://www.eere.energy.gov/consumer/tips/
Information about improving energy efficiency at home from the U.S. Department of Energy.

### UN Division for Sustainable Development

http://www.un.org/esa/sustdev/
Provides information about how the UN is working to encourage sustainable development around the world.

### Municipal Solid Waste—Reduce, Reuse, and Recycle

http://www.epa.gov/epaoswer/non-hw/muncpl/reduce.htm
Information about cutting down garbage from the U.S. Environmental Protection Agency.

### Organic Gardening

http://www.organic-gardening.net/
A guide to planning, starting, and maintaining an organic garden.

## Books

Bowden, Rob. *Waste*. San Diego: Kidhaven Press, 2004.

Green, Jen. *Waste and Recycling*. North Mankato, Minn.: Chrysalis Education, 2004.

Morgan, Sally. *Alternative Energy Sources*. Chicago: Heinemann Library, 2003.

Oxlade, Chris. *Energy: Present Knowledge, Future Trends*. North Mankato, Minn.: Smart Apple Media, 2005.

Richards, Julie. *Solar Energy*. North Mankato, Minn.: Smart Apple Media, 2004.

Stoyles, Pennie. *Global Warming*. North Mankato, Minn.: Smart Apple Media, 2003.

# Index

HERR MEMORIAL LIBRARY